The

Serial

Killer

Ministries

~While you're praying, they're preying~

Cornelius W. Dixon
2015

Dedication

This book is dedicated to my best friend and her daughter, Shantorrian & Xa'Miya. You're one of the most amazing friends I have. I thank God for you! You have been such a great friend, and I know God is about to do great things in your life!!

To little sister and brother; Mya & Zylon. You two mean so much to me, and are one of the reasons I try my hardest to make it to success, because when God blesses me; He'll bless you too! Just knowing you look up to me, I strive my best to be a great example for you! I LOVE YOU!!!

To my good friend Tyra Frazier, (author of Traveling through your storm); thank you for helping me in the moments I wanted to snatch my hair out and scream. You kept me calm and went out of your way to make sure this book had what it needed, and gave great wisdom and advice!

Table of Contents

Not everyone in church is praying for you!

Introduction

Everyday people become victims of senseless acts of murder. Someone taking one's life and even their own lives, is an everyday occurrence in this world. As I've watched TV over these past couple years, it seems like every time I turn around, someone has been raped, killed, fighting, and locked up. We've continued to pray for things to get better, yet it seems things are still turning for the worst.

In the midst of the cases we see on television, hear about on the radio, and read about on the internet, there is mass murder that has been going on for years now, and we never hear about it or notice it until it's too late. There is an UN-convicted serial killer (or killers) on the loose, and they are out to kill, steal and destroy; no one is safe. These killers are nothing like the typical murderers because they don't hide out until things blow over to make their next move. These murderers feed off the crowd and the more people who witness their plans unveiling, the more they have to showcase. The death is a long process; the victims cry out, they fight, they struggle to live and breathe. They are alive physically, but dead emotionally and spiritually. They are the serial killers of the church. They love to kill the vision of the church, the people, and their ultimate goal is to cause chaos in the body of Christ. Truth be told, they've been winning, and we are losing the battle that we should be winning.

1
The enemy among us

"From there it spies out the prey; its eyes observe from afar." Job 39:29

Just because you're at church, does not mean you're at church. You may be in the building; yet your heart, mind, and spirit is not actively participating in true worship. Because, true worship constitutes a lifestyle and a mentality to support it. Sadly in today's world, we have a lot of people at church, but they are not in church. They come into the house not to praise God, receive the word, and fellowship among the body. They come in to cause chaos and sow seeds of discord among the brethren, and we never really notice them. We have to wake up and realize that the enemy can and will come through the church as well, and if we are not careful and prayerful we will find ourselves fighting a battle we can't win simply because of our focus is off.

Understand this, the enemy is watching your every move. He knows your struggles and he designs things and people and purposely sets them in your path to push your buttons and try and knock you off course. His goal is to destroy the ministry and infect the body and cause it to not be effective. A lot of times you will find that your worst enemy will be the ones who sit in the same pews as you.

Job 1:6-7 gives reason to believe that the enemy is watching you, not just at home, school, or on the job, but in the house of God as well. Let's look at the scripture and deal with it deductively.

...

Job 1:6, "Now there was a day when the sons of God came to present themselves before the Lord, and Satan also came along with them."

Cornelius W. Dixon

...

Theologians give two very profound scenarios that could possibly be going on in this portion of the story of Job. One natural and one spiritual. I believe they both are very befitting to our lives today. So let's discuss them and see the relevance to our lives spiritually and naturally. Now, the scripture gives us a distinct setting in which the event take place where it says, "There was a day when the sons of God came to present themselves before the Lord".

...

Spiritually: This could mean a time in the spiritual realm where the angels (known as the sons of God) presented themselves in the presence of the Lord, and Satan (a former angel) came along with them.

...

Naturally: This could mean times in which the true saints (the sons and daughters of God) assembled themselves together to go into the presence of the Lord, and Satan, (an enemy, hypocrite, one who has a form of Godliness and denying the power thereof) was also in the midst of them to distract and hinder.

...

I believe both of these scenarios are things we face when dealing with the spiritual assassins in the church. Here is why. The natural and mental battles we fight are manifestations of the warfare in which is going on in the spiritual realm. Consider Ephesians 6:12,

...

Eph. 6:12, "For we wrestle not against flesh and blood, but against principalities, against powers, against the rulers of darkness of this world, against spiritual wickedness in high places. (KJV)"

...

The enemy has proposed war in the spirit, and we sometimes experience the chaos in our natural lives. What is going on here in the text? The sons of God (Sons, daughters, and angels) come together at appointed times to present themselves in the presence of the Lord, and Satan comes along with them. Notice here that Satan had not been recognized, identified, or confronted of his presence until Jesus acknowledged Satan was there

My question is, why did no one recognize Satan was there? Which leads me to believe that, first of all, just because we go into the church and the spirit of God falls, it doesn't stop Satan from coming into the presence. The reason we may not notice him is because he looks, speaks the scriptures, and acts like us as a camouflage. I don't care how long you have been saved; the enemy is watching. I don't care what church you go to and how long you've been going; the enemy is still there. No matter how high you praise, how long you preach, you can speak the deepest tongues in the Christian faith; the enemy is still among us and he's trying to distract and hinder you from going forward in God. Now let's look back at the text.

...

Job 1:7, "And the Lord said to Satan, 'From where do you come?' So Satan answered the Lord and said, "From going to and fro on the earth, and from walking back and forth on it"

...

Satan has been recognized by Jesus (shout there because the Lord knows the enemies among you) and Satan tells him that he has basically been walking throughout the earth, so let's go into the next chapter to discuss what Satan is doing on his journey.

Cornelius W. Dixon

2
The Strategy Room

"Be sober, be vigilant; because your adversary the devil walks about like a roaring lion, seeking whom he may devour." 1 Peter 5:8

The adversary has been watching you. He studies your every move. He and his demons are taking record of every event of your life in hopes to hinder and destroy you and your dreams. Sadly, most of the time, we see this going on in the church. The enemy knows exactly what buttons to push. He knows your weakness and the desires of your flesh, and he sends forth obstacles to cause you to stumble. Your dreams and visions, and the anointing of God on your life causes the enemy to tremble. So he uses the data he records to design people and things to knock you off course.

In Job, Satan says that he has been walking all throughout the earth, and it is here that Peter picks up on and exposes the enemy's agenda. He begins by encouraging us to be "sober" and "vigilant" (meaning: to be alert, careful, watchful and temperate at all times) because the enemy is lurking. He then uses the illustration of the devil walking about as a "roaring lion" What is the significance of that? Simply put, the lion's roar is used as communication with the rest of the pride. Satan as a roaring lion as he lurks around and watch you, roars as communication to the rest of his pride (demons) giving them the status update with you. By him lurking and communicating with the demons he begins planning and plotting against the people.

Paraphrase, Job 1:8 The Lord asks Satan, "Have you considered my servant Job" and Satan replies, "Yes, but Job don't fear for no reason, you got a hedge around him; but if you remove I can make Job curse you to your face." The reason the enemy is allowed to even confront you, is because God has enough faith in you to know that even in the midst of hell you can withstand. Yet a lot of times we fail in that moment because our focus has been on our things, and not the one who has blessed us with it. Can God brag on you, and can you stand even when your life is under the scope?

...

Luke 22:31-32, And the Lord said, "Simon, Simon! Indeed Satan has asked for you, that he may sift you as wheat. But I have prayed for you, that your faith should not fail; and when you have returned unto me, strengthen your brethren."

...

Brothers and sisters, the enemy has watched you and inquired of you to sift you.

...

John 10:10, "The thief does not come except to steal, and to kill and to destroy…"

...

He desires to steal every potential growth, to kill all hopes and dreams, and destroy every vision to keep you from bringing glory to God. What do you do?

...

1 Peter 5:9, "resist him, steadfast in the faith, knowing that the same sufferings are experienced by your brotherhood in the world."

...

Simply put, stand firm in God and resist the enemy, keep the faith. After all, you're not the only one who has experienced, is experiencing, or shall experience at a future time, these very sufferings.

So as God gives Satan our address and the permission to attack all that he can, he doesn't have permission to take our lives. Satan calls for a board meeting with his demons to design devices and a strategy to kill us. He doesn't take our natural lives, but he hires spiritual assassins to kill us spiritually and emotionally.

Cornelius W. Dixon

3
The Thrill of the Kill

"They have now surrounded us in our steps; they have set their eyes, crouching down to the earth, As a lion is eager to tear his prey, and like a young lion lurking in secret places." Psalms 17:11-12

Satan takes great pleasure in killing the saints. Just to watch you struggle and suffer makes him feel great. We cannot give him the pleasure of doing so. He's like those who hunt with passion, getting a thrill out of the killing of their prey. He does not ultimately kill you physically; he uses others around you to kill you emotionally and spiritually. They are called the spiritual assassins. What do spiritual assassins do? They come up against you to choke the life

out of your potential, your dreams, the
ministries and visions you have for your life
spiritually and naturally. Spiritual murder
happens every day. This murder is the worst
kind because the victim remains alive while
spiritually dead. They have no life inside of
them. They have no hope and no faith. They
are like the bones in the book of Ezekiel.
After he has prophesied to them and the
bones came to their respective places and
the skin, tendons, and sinews came upon
them; they stood up yet still had no life.

Most of the time you find people who
kill others dreams are those who have no
dreams for themselves, or recognize the
greatness in others and become intimidated.
They become intimidated because they feel
like you will become greater than them or
"out do" them, and not thinking that if
we're working for God we are all on the
same team, and there is no one greater than
the Father.

As I began to think of this subject, I
began to think about the parable of the

wheat and the tare. God showed me a few things in the text as it relates to our lives and the spiritual murders that often occur through the church. Let's look at the scriptures and deal with them deductively. The scriptures can be found in Matthew 13:24-30.

...

Matthew 13:24, Another parable He put forth to them saying: "The kingdom of heaven is like a man who sowed good seeds into his field; but while men slept, his enemy came and sowed tares among the wheat and went his way."

...

In this text the man sowed good seeds in the field. But while they slept and didn't stand guard, the enemy came among them and sowed tares among the crop. What does this relate to? Sunday after Sunday we come to church hearing the word of God; we attend bible study and learn more about God and his word that is relative to our lives, yet there are times we lose focus or we fail to use discernment and that's when the enemy decides to come and set up obstacles in the way. We have to continue to watch and not allow the enemy to step in and mess up the good seeds that we have sown. We are human and makes mistakes, and the enemy will use them to get into your territory. I've always been taught that "Sin lies at the door, and the devil waits for an opportune time". What happens next?

...

Matthew 13:26-27, "But when the grain had sprouted and produced a crop, then the tares also appeared. So the servants of the owner came and said to him, 'Sir, did you not sow good seed in your field? How then does it have tares?"

...

The enemy has come into the church, and our lives and has sown tares among the harvest. We have allowed so many of the enemy's spirits to come in and take position in the church and have given him so much opportunity. He has set up so many stumbling blocks and when we look at our lives and look at the condition of the church we go to the master and ask, "How did it get like this"? Watch this closely. The text says that when the wheat had begun to sprout then the tares began to appear. When the potential begins to grow or the vision begins to manifest, that's when the enemy and his devices begin to manifest to choke out the potential that is trying to grow. When the enemies in the church begin to see your growth they begin to do or say any and everything to hinder it from growing.

...

Matthew 13:28-29, "He said to them, 'an enemy has done this.' The servants said unto him, 'Do you want us then to go and gather them up?' But he said, 'No, lest you gather up the tares you also uproot the wheat with them. Let both grow together until the harvest, and at the time of the harvest I will say to the reapers, "first gather together the tares and bind them in bundles to burn them, but gather the wheat into my barn."

...

I've ministered from this scripture before and my question to the church was, "What do you do when your enemies are worshipers too"? Truth is, the serial killers will always be among us, but you don't have to fall victim to them or try and fix the situations on your own. Why did the owner tell the servants not to try and remove the wheat? Because there was a potential that they may gather tares among the wheat. So he told them to just let them grow together. Even though the enemy is lurking around you there is still a possibility for you to grow. Don't allow the presence of opposition in your life hinder you from growing and choke the very life out of your spirit. He said let them grow, and at the time of harvest I will do the separating.

The tares and wheat look alike. You cannot tell what is what just by looking. So,

Cornelius W. Dixon

how do you tell the tares from wheat? Early in the morning when the sun rises. The wheat bows in submission to the power of the sun, while the tare lifts up its face in rebellion. You can notice the serial killers in the church because even in the presence of God they lift up rebellion and trouble, while the saints are submitting to the presence and authority of the Son.

4

When You Pray, You're Prey

"Therefore all those who devour you shall be devoured; and all your adversaries, every one of them, shall go into captivity; those who plunder you shall become plunder, And all who prey upon you I will make a prey." Jeremiah 30:16

Look around, not every on who comes to church and sits next to you is actually standing in agreement with you or praying for you! There is no hurt like church hurt. There are some people who are influenced by Satan to set forth opposition in your life.

Cornelius W. Dixon

When you gave God your life and made up your mind to run for Jesus, you became a target for the enemy and his assassins. Just as a lion quietly lurks in the grass waiting to kill, so it is in the spirit. The devil lurks around waiting on the opportunity to pounce on you; you're his prey. If he can stop your prayer life he knows it's just a matter of time until you give in to him. You may think, "Well I thought praying was supposed to push the devil away"! You're right. It can and it will, but only for a season. The higher you go in God, the more you have to fight. As you begin to experience new levels there are new devils to wage war against.

People of God, don't be fooled. There is an enemy in every church. They can sit anywhere from the pulpit to the exit doors. Some wear titles, some can sing and pray till you get happy, and still be so full of hell. People have become so competitive in the church. When you want to operate fully in the great gifts God has blessed you with, there are people who will come against you. Their purpose is to come against every move you make. They will do anything and say anything to keep you from flowing. They won't participate or support your programs, and they won't always agree with the song you sang or how you sang it.

Your dreams and visions are not good enough if they're not theirs. They will try and turn others against you and what you're trying to do. They seem to be the biggest critics of the church, and think their opinions are powerful enough to stop what God is doing in your life. The only way they can stop it is if you let them. They prey mainly on the weak ones. Those who want to do right, but lack in boldness or have self-esteem issues. Everyone won't like you or agree with you, but you cannot allow that to stop you from going. As long as you know God said do it, keep pressing and don't allow anyone or anything to hold you back from walking in purpose.

Cornelius W. Dixon

Romans 1 starting at verse 16-32 gives us a complete understanding of why they are like this and gives the results that are to come for them because of their mindset. Reading and understanding these scriptures can help you to identify some serial killers that have attached themselves to you and are trying to get close enough to strangle the life out of your spirit. Everyone, from the beginning of time, was created with a purpose and destiny and God gave all of us gifts to operate for His glory. There are people who have operated in these gifts and have become so prideful that they failed or rejected giving God the glory and honor; and now they feel as if it's all about them.

So in a nutshell, Paul begins to tell us there is no excuse. These people knew God and didn't glorify him or praise him sincerely. They became foolish and self-righteous and their hearts became darkened. They began to change the glory of God for themselves and are so into what they have, what they can physically see or touch and

have corrupted what is supposed to be
incorruptible. Thus, God has given them up
to a reprobate mind so that they can fulfill
the desires of the flesh. Therefore, they walk
in the wickedness of the enemy instead of
the righteousness of God. As a result, they
continuously bring death to themselves. You
can identify them because they are the main
ones who approve of the wrong things
instead of standing up for what is right.
Instead of walking in truth, they allow the
lies to have dominion over their thoughts.

Isn't it funny how a group of individuals
who sometimes don't even like each other,
can come together in unity to tear down
someone else? They are lacking in God and
they see you trying to love everybody and
live holy. They will come together with
others just to try and trap you. Let's look at a
few groups within the serial killer's ministry
that we seem to notice every day in the
church.

These groups have been birthed through
the unrighteousness of their own spirits.

Cornelius W. Dixon

After God gave them up to a debased and simplistic mind, they were not able to conceive righteous thought and they did things wrong that seemed right to them. Based on Romans 1:28-32, the next few chapters will be the things we see that are killing the church and the people that allow it to become a part of their everyday practices.

5
Sexual Immorality

"It is actually reported that there is sexual immorality among you, and such sexual immorality as is not even named among the gentiles-that a man has his father's wife!" 1 Corinthians 5:1

We all know that sexual immorality is abundant in the church today. We hear it and see it every Sunday, and for the sake of keeping members or fear of judging others we keep our mouths closed and just sweep it under the rug. Sweeping trash under the rug seems to be alright with us until it forms a hump and causes us to fall. When you are standing for what is right, it's not judgment.

Cornelius W. Dixon

Sexual immorality is killing the church by consuming the people who avail themselves too it.

When you are trying to like what is right, those who practice sexual immorality try to entice you to become a part of their lifestyle. You will find people using any and every mode to cause you to fall into sin. When you are weak in sexual aspects of your life, it is easy to fall into it. The serial killers of the church are spirits from hell that influence others to influence you. When the Bible tells us to connect ourselves with people of like, precious faith it's not saying that we can connect with everyone in the church, but rather find the ones who are beneficial to your growth. Connect with the ones who are trying to live the life which God says live, hold up the blood stained banner and stand up for holiness. They tempt you and cause you to fall into lust and lay with them. Let's discuss a few areas of sexual immorality that seem to be going on among the saints, and sadly the church is afraid to deal with them.

We have so many people committing sexual impurity in the church and it defiles the house. Instead of it being the house of prayer, it has turned into a big house of orgy and perversion. God is not pleased with this! Sexual immorality seems to be the strongest killer because everyone has a desire for sexual affection. Whether it be oral, intercourse, or masturbation; if it's not done right, its sin. Only the bed of marriage between man and wife is undefiled.

. . .

Homosexuality

We have seen this becoming an epidemic in the body of Christ today. People have begun to turn from the natural order of sex from the origins in which God intended. I've heard people saying, "I was born like this" or "God made me like this". Let's talk about this. First of all, who you decide to love is all your business, I have no heaven or hell to put you in, however, that's not how God wants you to be. I honestly believe that

Cornelius W. Dixon

a lot of people were born homosexual, and a
lot have been molested and raped and it
caused them to turn to that lifestyle.
Deliverance is needed, but there is no way
possible that God created you as a
homosexual. There is a difference in your
creation and conception. God created Adam
and built woman (Eve) for the man. Though
they were created perfect and sinless, the
devil entered in and tainted them. The
enemy has crept into the womb and planted
homosexual seeds into individuals and the
church.

That's why we are now seeing, "Pastor
and his First Gentleman" or "Pastor and
Her Elect Lady". It's not right, and those
who accept it and approve of it are just as
lost and confused as those who practice it.

...

Leviticus 18:22 "You shall not lie with
males as with a woman. It is an
abomination."

...

God does not approve of this lifestyle. Let us not forget Sodom and Gomorrah, they were destroyed for the practice of homosexuality. People have to understand that even if you're not homosexual, just because you approve it in others you cause the sin upon yourselves as well. You will hear men say "I'm not gay, but I do like girl on girl action." You're still wrong!

It's not that we can't associate ourselves with them or push them away; we just can't become emotional, physical, or spiritual partakers of the lifestyle. They can come to church yet don't put them in leadership positions. It's not the place for them. It's not just homosexuality, it is more that we will discuss in the latter portions of this book. So how is the spirit of homosexuality considered a serial killer of the church? It enters the body and not only influences a person, but it also causes that person to act as if it's right. They will try to get you to approve or even join in and if you're not careful you will fall into the trap.

Cornelius W. Dixon

We have adopted this into the church because society says it's right. We begin to give them titles. No, this is not how God wants it. Let's move on.

• • •

Adultery

Adultery is another sexual impurity that runs through the church. It is sometimes unacknowledged and undetected. You watch the news and hear reports all the time of disputes going on in church, because the spouse has had or is having an affair. Preachers are sleeping with their members and the members are sleeping with each other. Even the very thought of having sex with someone other than your spouse is considered adultery.

These are serial killers, because they also try to entice you. Now, the vows spouses make at their wedding has no meaning, because as soon as sister "thick" and brother "so sexy" start feeling some type of way, they try to seduce you into the bed. The church has become the hook up spot to find your sideline partner or friend with benefits. God doesn't honor that!

It's not just stepping outside of your own home that causes adultery. Even if you are separated or divorced and you take on another partner it is still adultery. Unless that spouse is divorced because of infidelity or separated by death, it is adultery. (Read Matthew 5:32). Yet, we allow them to be leaders of the church. We have begun to pervert and contaminate things that God has deemed to be holy and have corrupted that which God has deemed to be incorruptible. When a person commits sexual impurity, they not only sin against God, but also sin against their own bodies. Those who practice these things attack your marriage and your home. The next killer we find is:

. . .

Fornication

This is something we all have been tempted to do or have done. When you find yourself trying to have sex out of wedlock and see nothing wrong with it, and continue in it, it begins to consume you. Sex is meant for marriage and that only. There are fornicators who try and seduce you and bring you into sin. These are killers because the enemy is trying to contaminate you in every way he can to kill any possibility of you walking in the spirit and fulfilling the purpose that God has given you. The devil knows what you desire in a man or woman, and he will send people in the church that look like what you want as a trap to try and capture you. You have to stand firm in faith. All in all, we will be tempted, but with the temptation God will give us a way of escape.

6

Wickedness

**"Lord, how are they increased that trouble me!
Many are they that rise up against me. Many there
be which say of my soul, there is no help for him in
God." Psalms 3:1-2 (KJV)**

There are many people who come to church just to start trouble. They are messy, petty, and obnoxious. They sow seeds of discord among the brethren. They cause division in the house and we know a house that is divided of itself will fall. That's something you see in a lot of churches. People are wicked and attack people emotionally and spiritually just because they are simple minded and miserable.

Cornelius W. Dixon

People come to the house of God with
drama. They desire to do this among the
church, because drama is no good without
an audience. Spiritually, drama means,
"Designed reproaches against my
anointing" (Dr. Yvonne Capehart). Wicked
people in the church are serial killers
because they are the ones who attack people
to kill their spirit. They change people's
moods with their negative attitudes and their
foolish ways. They are the people who don't
know how to speak to a person without
doing or saying something offensive and out
of order. They are always complaining and
saying what they would or would not do in
situations that have nothing to do with
them. They have no life outside of hurting
others.

People like this will grieve you, make
you uncomfortable, annoy you, and make
you want to lose your mind. David says Lord
its too many people here that begin to
trouble me, and they rise up against me
(Psalms 3). They always seem to have their

opinions of my life in areas that only
Concern me and God. No one likes a "know
it all". Dream killers are conceited and
arrogant people, who always seem to have
something to say. They are so quick to speak
and never take time to listen. They always
say what you can't or will never do. They
have a form of Godliness, but deny the
power thereof. They have been washed in
water and not the blood. Like my grandma
said, "People have gone into the water a
devil and got up a wet devil."

Wickedness has spread through the
church. When I studied this part of serial
killers in the church, I was reminded of Eli
and his sons in the bible. 1 Samuel teaches
that the sons of Eli were wicked and
because of their wickedness the Ark of the
Lord was stolen. As a result of the ark being
stolen the presence of God had been taken
away. Then they were killed. One of the
son's wives went into premature labor and
died giving birth. The child's name was
Icabod (which means "Where is the glory")

and then Eli fell backward from his porch broke his neck and died. Wickedness brings death and causes the glory to be lifted. Don't allow anyone's foolishness to take you out of the presence of God. It's the only place you can be sane.

When you have the determination to praise God in the midst of your enemies, you take the power away from them. One of my favorite biblical stories is about Jehoshaphat and the people of Judah and Jerusalem (2 Chronicles 20). They received word that a multitude had assembled to come and fight them. Jehoshaphat began to fear and positioned himself to seek the Lord. The army that came against them (the people of Moab, Ammon, and Mount Seir) were people who didn't even like each other, yet they came together to destroy one person and his people. You have to be a powerful vessel to see enemies come together with their enemies just to destroy you. God told them don't fight the battle, let Him fight. Don't fear what the situation looks like, just go through it and allow God to show you His greatness. The day of the battle, Jehoshaphat sent out the praise and worship team before he sent out the army. Then as they began to sing and play, the Bible said the enemies ambushed themselves and destroyed each other and the people of Jerusalem arose to a place overlooking the wilderness and saw that their enemies had been destroyed. Your praise will confuse your enemies. So, when they try and silence you, continue to praise even louder. Why? If you are redeemed of the Lord, you ought to say something!

Cornelius W. Dixon

7
The Gossipers

"And besides they learn to be idle, wandering about from house to house, and not only idle but also gossips and busybodies, saying things which they ought not." 1 Timothy 5:13

I think it's safe to say that there are some motor mouths in the church. People love to talk and can't seem to mind their own business. Gossipers can take one thing they heard and run with it. They add things and take things away to cause others to look or react to you differently. The gossipers can take your testimony of how God changed your life and tell the struggle, but not speak on the deliverance. I can testify about sleeping with a married woman and things getting out of hand with that situation and how I had to go before God to repent and be restored. They don't tell of the repentance and restoration, all they will say is, "Oh he's supposed to be a preacher but he slept with a married woman." Not all rumors the gossipers tell are lies, some are the truth. When you decide to go tell how I slept with someone's wife, be sure to tell how I repented and allowed God to restore me and change me. People love to talk about your dirt, but fail to mention that God has already swept it up and threw it out with the other garbage.

It's really easy to point out the gossipers in the church. I like to call them by name. "Bro. He Said", "Sis. She Said", "Mother They Said", "Deacon I-Heard", and "Bishop If Only". That's how they identify themselves. He said this, she said that. They told me this, and I heard that, and if only you knew what he said, she said, they said and I heard.

Honestly, forget all the mess are they talking about and tell me what you said! We all encounter the gossipers. They throw rocks and hide their hands. They will be the main ones in your face talking about, "praise the Lord Saints" yet behind your back; talking in other people's ear about what they think they know. Me personally, when I come to church the last thing I need is another "Christian" burdening me with their opinions. We have enough to deal with in our everyday lives without allowing people to bring more. When I come to church, I desire it to be a W.O.W experience. W.O.W means "Worship over Worry!" Gossip, this has become spread throughout the church, and it's an infectious disease. The works thereof produce no productivity.

. . .

Back-Biters

These are people who feel the need to talk bad behind a person's back. They defame your character until they're in your face and then it's a whole different story. They are two faced and double minded. They try and ruin your reputation and name among the people who may be fond of you! If they have to go behind your back to talk, they are not even worth the time to confront. Save that breath as use it to praise God. I will tell you why at the end of this chapter.

. . .

Slanderers

These are the gossipers who make stuff up. They talk just to hear themselves talk. They're liars. They seem to wake up plotting what lie they can tell that day. They are a stumbling block, always trying to get you caught up in a scandal. Yes, it's in the church. Preachers, members, deacons, ushers, whatever position there is, there can be a slanderer. Preachers slander preachers, churches slander other churches. What happened to the realness of church? We've strayed so far away from how God desired for the church to be. It's not everybody in the church. However, it's becoming a majority and we wonder why people can't get a breakthrough and sinners don't want to come in. Why should they come in when they can find the same thing in the streets? The difference is, in the streets they get it free and in church you pay offerings. Anyone wanting God for real doesn't want to come to a church and pay somebody to talk about them.

• • •

Haters

I remember a song I liked in my childhood days that said, "Players gonna play, them haters gonna hate". When the Lord starts blessing you, you find out who's really for you! When God starts working in your life, people love to bring up, "what you used to do" or "who you used to be"! Let the haters hate! They just see the greatness in you and want to try and stop what God has started. They fail to realize "…He who has begun a good work in you will complete it until the day of Jesus Christ;" I see it like this, when people hate on you for what God is doing in your life they are really hating on God for choosing you! So, in spite of all the he say, she say, they said and I heard that goes on, you consider what God has said! What has God said concerning you and the gossipers?

…

Psalms 1:4, 6, "4. The ungodly are not so, but are like the chaff which the wind drives away. 6. For the Lord knows the way of the righteous, but the way of the ungodly shall perish."

...

Let fools be fools, only simple minded people walk in ignorance. They talk about what they don't know because their minds are too simplistic to handle the awesomeness of God and the revelation in which he shows through you! What else does God say?

...

James 1:26 "if anyone among you thinks he is religious, and does not bridle his tongue but deceives his own heart, this one's religion is useless."

...

Remember these serial killers have been turned over to a reprobate mind. They don't even know how wrong they are. Therefore, their religion is useless. They knew right from wrong, and refused to act accordingly, so God took it. Now, we can go on and on with scriptures about gossipers and all these other things we've discussed. But let's look at more of the church serial killers.

One of the saddest things I've seen in the church is people hating the members and the pastor; yet they keep going to that church. My question is, why go to a place if

Cornelius W. Dixon

you don't like the people there, especially if you don't like the pastor? How can you sit under someone that you have something against?

8
Maliciousness

"Hatred stirs up strife, but love covers all sins" Proverbs 10:12

Now, I can honestly say that a lot of the malicious acts you find against an individual or ministry comes from someone who is hurting. Having malice in your heart causes many other sub-spirits to enter in and operate in your life. So, when someone wrongs you, don't repay them in any way other than love. Not everyone is able to get to that point. That's when they begin to turn into the malicious ones. You have to realize that God will handle the situation and you just keep on loving that person. Maybe, just maybe, love was all they needed to wake them up. Some people act the way they act because it's all they know. It's all that has

Cornelius W. Dixon

been done to them. There are others who operate out of spite, and purposely try to harm the individual or ministry, and specifically target them. What do these types of actions display?

. . .

Envy

Envy is one reason behind malicious acts in the church. You go to church (sometimes, the same church) and are supposed to worship the same God and read the same word. What God has done and is doing for and with me, He can do the same for you. His word says that He is no respect of persons. The only difference is what God has for me, it is for me and what God has for you is for you! The same blood that was shed for you was shed for someone else. There is no reason to hate on or be jealous of anything another person has! No one will be jealous of someone who doesn't have something they want. When a person envies you, they most likely see something in you that you don't even see in yourself. When a person operates through a spirit of jealousy and envy, then it produces a spirit of:

...

Strife

My pastor often says, "If you stay in your lane, there won't be any accidents." Too many times we find people clashing and having bitter disputes with others because of envy and strife. People have started fighting in the church, and this kills the spirit and desire to even attend church. Churches these days are so full of drama and God is really not pleased. Most of the time, the envious ones are mad at the way God is blessing the true worshipers. I can think back now about situations I've seen in the church as a child. Back then I didn't know what was happening, but now that I'm older I can identify the spirits of envy and strife at play.

People become envious over other's positions, offerings, relationships with other members, and their gifts, ETC. It may sound weird, but it is real. It causes division and animosity among the brethren. In the spirit of strife people often then adopt the spirit of:

...

Deceit

I am pretty sure that you have seen deceitful people operating in the church. Some are just operating under an Antichrist spirit. Deceit is when a person holds back on facts or misrepresents the truth; usually done to make themselves seem as if they're right or to look good. Walking in deceit is an individual's aim to mislead. Some preachers do it every week, misleading the people and concealing the truth. The spirit of deceit is another thing that is running wild throughout the body of Christ. All of these things we have talked about not only spiritually kill the members, but make the entire body suffer as well, causing people to become lost.

• • •

Rebellion

Rebellion is a sin of witchcraft. Rebellion has also run rampant in the church. No one wants to be told what to do and corrected. According to Romans 13:1, people have forgotten that we are to submit ourselves to higher authorities. When you find people rebelling against the man or woman of God, they are rebelling against God, against His word, against His counsel, and will definitely be destroyed through their acts of rebellion. So many people think they can do what they want, when they want, however they want and fail to realize that God has a way of doing things. I somewhat blame the leaders for not standing boldly in the church, because if we continue to pat sin on the back and not deal with it, it further creates a problem.

···

Hebrews 12:8 (KJV), "But if ye be without chastisement, whereof all are partakers, then are ye bastards, and not sons."

···

Picture this: Your child continues to do the wrong thing and you never correct them and they seem to get the idea that what they are doing is correct. When someone comes to them and corrects them, they immediately begin to become defensive and disrespectful, because you didn't deal with the problem when it first manifested. When we fail to rebuke, reprove, and restore order in the church we are nourishing bastards and not saints. The word bastard, according to the bible, is not a person born out of wedlock or without a father, it is a person who does not want to adhere or submit themselves to authority. I don't care who you are, you are not above order. Neither are you above being corrected and rebuked.

We cannot allow rebellion to hinder the church anymore. It is a demonic spirit and a sin of witchcraft. We are to cast out demons and the bible says that God suffers witches to die and sorcerers to be burned. Keep on walking against the power of God, and you're going to find yourself being put to death and burning.

. . .

Covetousness

Some people are extremely spoiled. They want everything they see and if they don't get what they want, then they throw temper tantrums. These are immature saints. They think they can throw "hissy fits" when things don't go their way! Covetousness is a sin, and the Ten Commandments tell us that we are not to covet. Jealousy, envy, and idolatry also come as a result of this.

• • •

Greed

When you find a covetous person, they are operating in greed. They just have to have what they see. People will kill one another because of greed. They will try to stop another person from enjoying what they want. The main reason for greed in the church is authority and money. Everyone wants the abundance and everybody wants to be in charge. The love of money is so evident in the church, especially from the deacon board and the pulpit. The souls of the people have become irrelevant and all people seem to worry about today is the other person's wallet and pocket book.

• • •

Violence

Out of covetousness, greed, and other impure thoughts and actions births out violence. People will begin to beat up on the saints. They begin to verbally, mentally, and spiritually abuse people and sometimes physically.

9
Pride

"For I say, through the grace given to me, to everyone who is among you, not to think of himself more highly than he ought to think, but to think soberly, as God has dealt to each one a measure of faith." Romans 12:3

This is, no doubt, one of the most vicious killers of the body and the ministry in which it attaches itself to. Pride affects all of us in some manner. The church individually and collectively has become so arrogant and prideful in some things, that we seem to lose sight in God and how He wants to do things in us, for us, and with us. There is nothing sadder than to see than an arrogant, self-righteous, and egotistical Christian. My grandmother used a phrase about people in the church being so

"heavenly minded and no earthy good."
People fail to realize that the blessing you
have didn't come because you were some
awesome person, but because of God's
grace and mercy. You didn't reach this level
of success because of your title, degrees, or
bank account, but simply because God saw
fit to allow you to get here.

It makes me sick to come into the
church and see people with their nose up
and being petty. Just because someone
doesn't sing the way you sing, or dance the
way you dance doesn't make them any better
or worse than you. Just because I may not
have the clothes you have, been saved as
long as you have, or been a member of the
church as long as you have, doesn't make
my salvation any more or less real than
yours. The same blood that was shed for you
is the very same blood that was shed for the
other, so don't act as if you are too perfect to
experience a down season.

...

James 4:6, "But He gives more grace.
Therefore He says: 'God resists the proud,
but gives grace to the humble.'"

...

Understand this, God does not bless the prideful. You have to humble yourself. Do it willingly or God will do it for you. There was a time I felt that since I was saved that I didn't have to listen to anybody and that I was better than others. The word says that pride comes before destruction. While you are busy trying to tear others down with your prideful ways, God will quickly use it to tear you down. What are some attitudes we find in prideful people that identify them?

• • •

Arrogance

Arrogant people feel as if everyone wants to be like them and if you're not like them you're nothing. I know through experience. I have come in contact with so many preachers and singers that feel that if I am not like them then my ministry is worthless. If I don't preach as long or sing as high they feel I'm not real. Arrogance will block you from really walking in the anointing of God. It's not about you! When it comes to God we are all equal. We all have a purpose and we are required to walk in that. My pastor's group sings a song that

Cornelius W. Dixon

says, "I can only be who I am, I can only be me, I'm only what Christ has called me to be!" I don't have the time, or patience to be or try to be like anyone else. The vision of your life should not be that you become the best imitation or duplicate of another, but be the best you! There is only one you! Nobody can beat you at being you! Arrogance is abundant in the church, but remember if it had not been for the Lord, whether you acknowledge it or not, you would not be where you are today!

• • •

Conceit

Arrogance is always accompanied by conceit. People are acting as if they are the best at doing everything and cannot be taught. You know this is abundant in the church in every area. People feel like they're the best usher, the best preacher, or as if the only reason the church is like it is, is because of them. The church doesn't need that. I call those types of people the "Glory Stealers." God can't get the glory because you're too busy taking it for yourself. There is a difference in being conceited and confident. Confidence speaks of not allowing anyone or anything hinder the potential. Conceit speaks as no one else's potential matters, because you are the most important. Who are we to feel as if we are more important than others? The same God who gave us the potential is the same one who can make it non-effective.

• • •

Boasters

Where you find arrogance you find conceit. Where you find conceit, you will find boasting. People love to brag and be bragged on. They love to do things for a show and boast about what they have or have done. When you brag about what you have or have done, it takes away from God. People brag about money they have, what they have done for the church, or the people in it. People hardly ever do things behind the scenes out of love. They always want recognition for it. When you start bragging and wanting the praise for what you have done, then God sees no reason to reward you because you've already received your reward.

10
Religion

"These things indeed have an appearance of wisdom in self-imposed religion, false humility, and neglect of the body, but are of no value against the indulgence of the flesh." Colossians 2:23

Religion has become one of the most hindering spirits known within the church community. It not only attacks the people, but the ministry as a whole. It's mostly the leadership that take the punches when dealing with religious people. Religion is all right in some ways. When I speak of religion, I'm referring to people who are like the Pharisees and Sadducee. They were so religiously minded, yet they were unaware of the move of the spirit and the will of God being revealed before their eyes. They were so stuck on the law and didn't understand that the fulfillment of the law was walking around them every day. These people were scholars, they read and studied the scrolls, and preached in the temples day in and day out. They were so smart, yet they lacked wisdom of the spirit and walked in ignorance. They were fools. The very Messiah they preached and read about was right there in their faces. They called him a fake, because he didn't come how they imagined him to come or how they were taught that He'd come; they didn't believe. They could not understand or comprehend him. Why? They were full of religion, yet they lacked a very important ingredient; they lacked a relationship!

There is a difference between having religion, and having a relationship! Religion is so programmed, yet relationship is spontaneous. Religion is stubbornness, yet relationship is flexible and teachable. When Jesus told the disciples to go to the next city, He said there will be a full grown donkey and a baby colt, loose them and bring them. Both were loosed, but only the young colt was used. Why not use the full grown one? It's been broken and it knows the way as opposed to the baby. It has never been sat on by man. The older the donkey gets, the more it becomes stubborn and stuck in its ways, though the baby will be wild and buck when you get on it, it is trainable and will eventually submit itself.

God wants someone he can use. He does not want someone so stuck in their ways that they can't seem to let God have His way. Worship is supposed to be life changing and powerful. Praise is to be open, expressive, and liberating, but because of religion we are quieted and held back. Religion will say, "It doesn't take all of that" when relationship causes you to dance like David danced.

If the religious really understood the concept and benefits of relationship, then they would understand why you praise the way you do. When David's wife rebuked him for the praise he was giving to God, (her religious mindset toward the fact that he was the king) David's response was, "I'll become even more undignified than this" (because of his relationship). See, what religion fails to realize is, God has been too good not to praise Him, and the ones who have relationship understand that if they hold their peace, the rocks will cry out! When you see a person that is so religiously dedicated, yet lacking relationship, you ultimately find that they operate in the spirit of:

...

Tradition

Tradition is one of the most vicious killers of the ministry. The ministry's growth is hindered because of the traditions of man. Being open minded, I will say this, tradition is all right to observe sometimes, but when it becomes a hindrance to the flow of the spirit, then it needs to be dealt with. Traditions are passed down by families and ministries, and there is nothing wrong with having traditions as long as you allow God to show up and do what he wants to do and needs to do in them.

Traditional people will keep you from doing new things in the ministry. Tradition will keep you from going to the next level. So many times I've seen and heard people trying to block others from moving forward. "We don't do it like this!", "My grandma did it like this!" Let's be real about it. When I see God wanting to do a new thing, wanting to send forth a fresh anointing, and a fresh wave of his spirit, I could care less about your traditions.

So excuse me ma'am, and pardon me sir. I don't care about your grandmother raising you in this church, I don't care that your granddad bought the first brick, and your uncle Pookie put the first nail in the wall, when it comes to me doing what God says do, get out of my way!

For too long we have been held back by the traditions of men. Traditional people will honor God with their lips, yet their hearts be far away from him. They are more committed to how "Grandma did it" and not how God wants you to do it. It's not that grandma was wrong, it's just that God may be wanting you to do it a different way.

Don't be as those people who worship in vain and teach traditions as if it were the Gospel of Christ!!

...

Mark 7:13, "Making the word of God of no effect through your tradition which you have handed down. And many such things you do."

...

The traditions of man have made the word of God of no effect in our lives. How can the promises the word gives us manifest, when you hold traditions to a higher standard than the word of God? It's not the new things that come in that defile the body of Christ, it's the things that have already been here that have caused the church to become contaminated! Who are you to get upset just because God wants to do something through someone you are not used to, or do something in a different way? You shouldn't be as long as it's a move of God.

So many people have left the church because of tradition, and people not wanting to receive change. Instead of them going to another church, they sit at home angry and bitter! Saints, some of us need to GROW UP! We need to stop throwing tantrums like little kids! When my daughter has tantrums she gets spanked and she straightens up! Don't make God have to whoop you to get you in line! It's dangerous for us not to move forward. Why must we stay in an elementary state of mind when

God is trying to elevate us to college level saints?

Answer this question: What is the difference between devotion and praise and worship? Only the style of it, yet when done sincerely, both will usher in the spirit of God. In both services, you sing, read scripture, and pray. It's the same thing. It's just done a different way and accomplishes the same goals. However, the traditional ones will say, "praise & worship is not how my great grandma'nem used to do it." or "all these new songs are nothing, the old school is the real deal." Don't get me wrong, I love old school gospel, but I don't think it is any less powerful than SOME OF THE NEW! Yes, I said some. If you think about it, a lot of these new songs are just old songs with a new style.

This generation has made praise & worship a tradition and will even tell you, "I'm not going to that church, devotion is too long." I do agree that there will be a time where you're going to have to call on the older songs. These new songs are great, but some have turned into more of a club song or love making song, rather than worship.

Listen, just because you have a nice beat and pretty melody and you say Jesus a few times in the song doesn't make it praise and worship. Even the devil will sing about Jesus but his heart is not in it. The spirit didn't conceive it!

Don't allow man-made traditions block you from moving in the outpouring of the Holy Ghost. If the tradition is allowing God to do a new thing, by all means celebrate it, but if it's a stumbling block, RUN! Tradition will block the promises of God and deliverance. Tradition is so caught up in the program, but as my pastor says "Deliverance is not printed on the program!" The best program, is no program. Let God have his way! Be it popular or not, let God move!

Cornelius W. Dixon

11
Lack of Order

"Let all things be done decently and in order."
1 Corinthians 14:40

I want to talk more about order in the church. Too many times, I have been in services and become so irritated because of out of order people and things. Listen, there is a place and time for everything. When you begin to operate in the wrong timing or in the wrong place, you're out of order. I went to Wal-Mart one day and I had to go to the restroom, when I went to the first stall; the sign on the door said, "Do not use, out of order," so I had to go to another stall. What does that have to do with the church? When you are out of order, and the spirit of God is searching for a vessel to use to send and release the power of God, God places a spiritual sign on your heart that says "out of order, do not use." If you wonder why God doesn't do anything for you or why you're not being as blessed as you should be, it's simply because you're out of order.

When there is a lack of order in the house of God, we allow the enemy access to the service. He uses the gaps to send in hindering and oppressing spirits to hinder the flow of God. Your actions are vital to the life of the service. I believe that everything that is said and done needs to be inspired by God and done decently and in order. We need order in the church so that our good deeds are not evil spoken of. We need order to keep hindrances from flowing in the church. A church without order, has no rule. That's why a lot of people fall into quarrels. If there were no lines in the road and signs to follow while driving, there would be no way to safely drive. Even with that, accidents do happen, but it's likely that someone over stepped the order and caused a collision.

We have to understand our boundaries, and be careful not to over step the boundaries. You over step boundaries when you go against the move of God, but also when you go against the leadership or set protocol of the house of God. You see this a lot when the people fail to submit to the leadership and other authoritative positions. What is the order and protocol of the local church?

God honors the law of order. If at any time a member acts out of order, it effects the rest of the body. If you have some type of pain or handicap in your body, then it causes the other parts of the body to have to carry the weight. Sometimes, one part of the body can be injured yet, it causes pain in multiple parts. It's not that it causes the other parts not to function, but it does cause them to strain or suppresses their production. So it is with the body of Christ. When you find yourself walking out of your position or calling or trying to take on the role of another office that's when you cause strain and in-productivity within the other body. That's why we are to stay in our lanes as I mentioned earlier.

The order of the church should line up in such a manner where the people are able to comprehend order. It is not that one office is more important than others because there are several auxiliaries that are all working together to achieve the ultimate goal: bringing God the glory, edification to the church, and winning lost souls for Christ.

...

God

God is first and foremost in the church. At least He should be. If you ever find a church that does not put God first GET OUT OF THERE! God is the head of the body, a body without a head is dead. If it is a real church, then it has to be governed by the one and true God, Jehovah! For without God, everything we do is pointless and void.

...

Pastor & Spouse

God as the head, uses a pastor to lead, shepherd, and father the congregation. They are in control of the church. They lead under the direction of God. If you ever find the pastor not being led by God, then that's not the place for you! Some pastors are so concerned about being liked and popular that they compromise authority and allow others to make vital decisions for them. As ministers of God, you cannot be weak and

Cornelius W. Dixon

fragile while leading people. You have to be bold and courageous. People will come against you to test you, but you have to stand firm and walk in the authority that God has given you, if you were actually called and ordained by God. I don't care who signed your license to preach, if it was not ordained of God, then the ministry is not real (and I will also say, going online to take a 5 minuet quiz to receive a license is not how God wants things done).

The pastor and spouse serve as the mother and father of the house. Just like in your household, the mom and dad make the decisions and provide the food for the children. If you ever find a pastor not ruling their own house then they surely won't be able to effectively rule the house of God. So many times there have been pastors out of place within the church, causing others to try and take on the role. To me, that is a spirit of anarchy. The pastor has to be in tune with God, for its the pastor that God gives the vision. Without God there is no vision, and without vision the people will perish (we will discuss lack of vision in a later chapter).

It's vital to have a pastor who walks and talks with God and lives the message they preach every day. Not that they won't make mistakes, for we all do, but God will hold them up if they follow Him. I love the way my pastor says it, "Follow me as I follow God!"

The church needs a preacher. Faith comes by hearing and hearing by the word of God. How can we hear without a preacher, even so, how can he preach unless he be sent? (Romans 10:17). So the preacher is very important to the body. However, notice this, the section heading is "Pastor and Spouse"; there is a relationship there. As a married pastor, the wife or husband is to be treated and respected equally. There should be no such thing as liking the pastor and hating the spouse! No, there is no way!

Often times you find the pastor's spouse being left out, when in all realness, when the pastor is struggling with hard headed members and other situations of the church, it is the spouse that has to comfort, encourage, and pray with them. The spouse is there when the pastor is up all night counseling members, studying, and writing sermons to feed the church. It is the spouse and the children who have to share their loved one with the church, even when they go without recognition. The divorce rates among preachers are ridiculously high because of conflict between the pastor's house and the pulpit.

As a married pastor, always remember your first priority is to your home, then the church! If it be any other way then you, pastor, are out of order! My pastor is a great inspiration for me, and a role model. I watch the relationship between him and his wife and daughters. He is a great example of how a pastor should be in the pulpit and at home. His motto is, "As long as my wife and the girls are happy then I am happy!" I want to be that type of pastor and husband that can take care of the church and my home. Then, I watch his wife and she shows me a great example of a first lady. If no one else prays for or encourages her husband, she will! She is his spiritual cheerleader! A spouse needs to stand by their partner in ministry, minister as a couple and allow God to be glorified. However, the pastor is still worthy of the wages! Don't muzzle the ox who treads the corn.

The pastor, as the head, has a very vital task simply because they have to be able to multitask. They have to take care of home, and serve as the brain, eyes, ears, and mouth of the church. A lot of times the roles of the pastor and the spouse go unappreciated and taken for granted, yet they come week after week to give you spiritual meals to enhance your Christian walk. This Sunday when you go to church, show the pastor and their spouse how much you love and appreciate them, and whatever you do let it be real and done out of love! When the pastor is blessed, you become blessed. The anointing runs from the top down. Don't miss your blessing by being out of order.

...

Leadership

These are the other leaders in office at the local church: ministers, evangelist, teachers, deacons and intercessors. They are what I call the neck, shoulders and hands of the church. They serve the purpose of supporting the pastor and spouse, and also doing work to support the vision. The pastor can't do everything; that's the purpose of having other leaders under them. The pastor cannot teach adult and youth bible study at the same time. The pastor can't teach intermediate, teen, and adult Sunday school at the same time. The pastor is not **GOD,** but a representative of God. The pastor is not omnipresent. Pastors cannot be in every place at one time! It is not your place to control the pastor or give ultimatums to the pastor. You are to be open and obedient to the needs of the ministry by request of the pastor. Also, let me rebuke this lie before I go any further: **DEACONS!** You are not the pastor, **NEITHER** do you have any authority over the pastor! I don't care how long you been saved or how old you are, **THE PASTOR IS THE PASTOR! GET IN ORDER!**

Your responsibility is to operate in your designated office and help take a load off the shepherd. You can be in places that the pastor can't at certain times. The pastor also needs a word and you should be able to minister on his behalf if called upon at any moment. That's why it's vital to stay in prayer and stay in the word because you can be called on even at the last minute. The leaders need to be in tune with God and the pastor so that they walk in sync, and in unity!

...

The Youth

The young people are being fought so hard in the world and the church to discourage them and push them away from the church. The serial killers in the church mainly target the youth because without the younger ones no one will be left when all the older people pass away. There is so much life, strength, greatness, and potential locked up on the inside of our young people. If the church doesn't stand up and take our babies back, they will be forever lost. I see the youth as the heart of the church. They are the thrive and the heartbeat. Young people are strong, and are willing to take risks and things like that. Stop allowing religiousness and traditional minded simplistic people to push our babies out of church! So what if they young? They are teachable. So what if they have problems, as all young people and older people do? They are still usable! Young people are different from most of the older ones. It may have taken the first verse of amazing grace to pull you in, but the young people may need something different!

If you get them in, teach them and guide them, there is absolutely nothing they can't or won't do for God. Stop judging these babies. Not all of them are sexually promiscuous, or disrespectful. There are some that want to be closer to God. Take them under your wings and teach them the standards of holiness. So what if her shorts are too tight? Teach her modesty. So what if his clothes are baggy? Teach him how to dress and act like a gentleman. It's the job for the older men and women of the church to teach the young folks. Some kids dress and dance the way they do because they have not been taught any better!

...

Lay Members

The rest of the congregation is the body from the chest down to the feet. They are the ones who support and carry the full ministry. They are the workers of the church. No one is more important than the other. We are all one body and every person is important. Yes, you find some being more faithful and doing more than some, and God will reward those. God gives leadership for the perfecting of the saints, so they can go out into the community and put into action the teaching they receive from the ministry leaders.

12
Lack of Prayer

"Watch and pray, lest you enter into temptation. The spirit indeed is willing, but the flesh is weak."
Matthew 26:41

Prayer is so vital to our Christian lives, not just individually, but as a church body as well. When we fail to have prayer in the church, the church begins to lose its power. Yes, we pray during devotion or praise and worship, pray over the offering, and pray at alter call; that's good. However, there needs to be a day where the saints gather together to pray throughout the church. Some of the most powerful services I have been in have been the result of fasting & prayer among the members, and having gate prayer (corporate prayer) before the service begins. Prayer before the service will set the atmosphere and bring such a tangible presence. If you pray before service, many times it will not be such a struggle to tap into the presence of God. However, in order for our prayer in the church to become strengthened, we have to have a steady prayer life at home. There is a saying: "NO prayer NO power, LITTLE prayer LITTLE power, MUCH prayer MUCH power."

In my first book, I wrote an outline of prayer, and I encourage you to read that book as well. However, listen, prayer does not always have to consist of you asking God for anything. In fact when you pray, don't automatically go in to ask for things. Sometimes your prayer should consist of you just giving God honor and glory for who He is, seeking His face and not just His hands. There is nothing wrong with asking God for things, but don't let that be the only reason you come to him.

They have taken prayer out of the schools and we have allowed prayer to become scarce in our homes and in the church. If we want to experience a move of God as on the day of Pentecost, we need to come together in prayer!

Cornelius W. Dixon

13
Lack of Vision
"Where there is no vision, the people perish: but he that keepeth the law, happy is he." Proverbs 29:18 (KJV)

A vision is needed. If you have no vision then what are you working for. With no vision, there is no mission. The vision is a goal and motivation for the church to work toward. Though opposition may come up there is potential there to achieve it as it has been given by God. If you just work toward the vision, God will give you provision to obtain the vision.

We need a vision. The vision doesn't die if we continue to work for it. Regardless of the stumbling blocks, the vision is yet! Though it tarry, wait for it. (Habakkuk 2). A pastor and congregation with no vision has no purpose and more than likely have not been established by God, therefore they labor in vain. When you have vision and you believe in the vision nothing or no one can stop you or block you from running to it.

Where there is no vision the people perish. Why is that? Where there is no vision, no one to teach and preach the word of God; and not in a traditional sense, but as of a prophetic sense, then the people perish; for there is no open vision. This means there is no productive message coming forth to edify the saints individually and collectively. The bible says man can't live by bread alone, but by every word that is continuously flowing from the mouth of God. Without the proceeding words of Christ the people are naked and open to shame and have no protective armor. Thus they are easy prey for the enemy. The people become idle minded, and open to play in sin and all these things, and they begin to perish for lack of knowledge. There has to be someone to teach the vision and prophetic words of Christ. The bible gives great encouragement and lesson and God's voice brings even greater revelation and inspiration.

Cornelius W. Dixon

14
Awake, Arise, &
Conquer

"Awake, awake! Put on your strength, O Zion; put on your beautiful garments, O Jerusalem, the holy city! For the uncircumcised and the unclean shall no longer come to you. Shake yourself from the dust, arise; sit down, O Jerusalem! Loose yourself from the bonds of your neck, o captive daughter of Zion! For thus says the Lord: 'You have sold yourselves for nothing, and you shall be redeemed without money." Isaiah 52:1-3

The church has been out of commission. It is time to awake from the sleep, arise to our rightful place, conquer the kingdom of darkness and let the glory of God be revealed. Though there are a lot of productive churches, there are others that are lacking and have allowed the demons of Satan to come in and take over. All churches of God regardless of the denomination are members of the unified body of Christ and we must all come together. First individually, then locally, and then collectively.

What is the problem? We're in the valley, dead and dry! God brought Ezekiel in the spirit to a valley full of dry bones, which represented the house of Israel (people of God). He asked Ezekiel, can these bones live? Ezekiel assessed the situation and by his reply you can imagine they were in pretty bad shape, so he answered, "Lord only you know!" God told him the great things He would do for them even in the midst of the valley, but before that could take place there was something else that had to take place, thus where our journey begins to awake, arise, and conquer!

...

Ezekiel 37:4-7, "Again he said to me, "Prophesy to these bones, and say to them, 'O dry bones, hear the word of the Lord! Thus says the Lord God to these bones: Surely I will cause breath to enter into you, and you shall live. I will put sinews on you and bring flesh upon you, cover you with skin and put breath in you; and you shall live. Then you shall know that I am the Lord.' So I prophesied..."

...

First thing we see happening is Ezekiel being obedient to the commandment of the Lord; in spite of what it looked like. He spoke life in the midst of a dead situation. The first step is for the leadership of the house. We have to learn to be obedient to God and speak life into what others may feel like there is no hope! Some of the problem has been the leader has been out of place. If the head is messed up, then the body will be messed up to. So even though they may seem like their potential for life is gone, you still have to speak the word through obedience. So Ezekiel said, "So I prophesied." What happened next?

...

Ezekiel 37:7, "...as I prophesied, there was a noise, and suddenly a rattling; and the bones came together, bone to bone."

As a result of the obedience of Ezekiel, he began to see an immediate manifestation of the promises of God. That is a wonderful thing. In order for us to receive manifestation of the promise, we have to be careful to obey God's command. So as he spoke the word, there came a sound. You know an awesome move of God is coming when you hear a sound. There are many scriptures that prove that when God began to manifest himself. The move of God is always preceded by a sound. When Elijah prayed for rain, before he saw any cloud or rain drops, he first heard a sound. When the spirit of the Lord fell on the day of Pentecost, when the people came together, the Bible said there came a sound. So, church, when we begin to come together and allow the move of God there comes a sound!

Not only was there a sound, he said there also was a rattling. Yes, I know rattling is also a sound, but it was a different type of sound. When something rattles, it means it's been shaken up! So, there came a sound and a rattling, and as I began to look at the text the Lord began to minister to me and said, "Tell my people, that this rattling, this shaking that is about to take place is a manifold manifestation!" My goodness! I heard the Lord say, "The shaking that is about to take place in the body of Christ, is Him shaking off the dust and the junk that we have come in contact with, shaking off the contamination!" He also said to me, "That when the enemy heard the sound, he became alert and began to tremble in fear, the rattling is also a sound of fear of the enemy beginning to tremble, because he knows that if the church would just come together; then there is a war about to go on, that he just cannot win!" I don't know who you are, but I want you to know that because God just spoke this thing, the enemy that has been seeking you is about to be defeated. Praise God for the sound!

There came a sound, a noise, and then the bones came together. They didn't just connect themselves to any available joint on whatever body. The King James Bible teaches that the bones came together, bone to his bone! The bones came to their respective place on the correct body. You know the song about the dry bones coming together. The bones connected. The Lord showed me that if we could just come together and get in place, in obedience to

His word, the order in the church will be restored.

The skeleton of the human body is the frame which gives the body its structure (its order). The body would not function if the toe bone was connected to the neck. The danger of having dry bones is the simple fact that if the bones are not moist, then it is not able to handle the pressure or the weight that comes with the body. However, if the bones are moist, they will be able to bend and strengthen themselves to carry the weight. If they are dry, they become more fragile and easy to break when pressure is applied. What else happened?

...

Ezekiel 37:8, "Indeed, as I looked, the sinews and the flesh came upon them, and the skin covered them over..."

...

As Ezekiel continued in watch, he saw the sinews, flesh, and skin cover the body. The sinew represents the tendons of the body. Tendons give the body mobility. The tendons activate the nervous system and allows the body parts to function as it should. The flesh represents the muscular system which gives the body the strength and ability that is needs. The skin is the outer layer that protects and covers the tissue on the inside of the body. These three have significant meaning. When we restore order in the church, God gives us mobility and strength and covers us in His protection. When all this came together they gained the ability to be identified. But, that's not all!

...

Ezekiel 37:8-10, "But there was no breath in them. Also He said to me, Prophesy to the breath, prophesy, son of man, and say to the breath, Thus says the Lord God: Come from the four winds, O breath, and breathe on these slain, that they may live. So I prophesied..."

...

The bones looked alive, but they had no life. There are a lot of people who know how to look or dress like saints, but they have not the spirit in them. There are churches that look and sound like church, but there is no life being given or experienced. So it's not enough to look the part that you don't live. I see this as having a "form of godliness", yet denying the power thereof. I don't care how well you dress or how great you shout, without the breath of God you're still dead. So again he prophesied and as he prophesied this happened:

...

Ezekiel 37:10, "...the breath came into them, and they lived..."

When the breath came into the slain, they lived. This is the awakening. We need the spirit to dwell in the church and in our homes that we may awake and live! Then watch this. After the breath came in, they awoke:

...

Ezekiel 37:10, "...and stood upon their feet..."

...

They began to arise. When you wake up, get up! There is no reason to continue to lay in the mess we've been delivered from. What did Ezekiel see after the bones woke up and stood up?

...

Ezekiel 37:10, "...an exceedingly great army."

...

He saw them as God intended them to be, an exceedingly great army. How do we become that? The bones came together to their individual bodies first, to represent the coming together of the local church, but here we see that it's more than one body. To become an exceedingly great army and conquer the enemy, we have to come together as the unified body of Christ! What does this mean? Regardless of race, denomination, or any other boundaries we face, we as the church body have to come together. When the blacks can worship with whites and we worship with other races and ethnic backgrounds, then we can arise and conquer. When the Baptists can connect with the Pentecostal and we connect with the COGIC (church of God in Christ) and other denominations, then we can conquer. Stop praising your denomination so much and feeling like your church is the only true church. God has other sheep in many different fields. We all serve the same God and we read the same Bible. How do we conquer as a unified body? When we come together in unity, God is glorified and the enemy becomes terrified. When we come together in unity, we come together in power! How great it is that the brethren can dwell among each other in unity! If one can chase 1000, and two can put 10,000 demons to flight, how much more do you think we can conquer with the entire body in unity and working in their respective places.

...

Ezekiel 37:13-14, "...You shall know I am the Lord...I have opened your graves...and brought you out...I will put my spirit in you...you shall live...then you shall know that I, the Lord, have spoken it and performed it..."

...

AWAKE, ARISE, AND CONQUER!

15
You're under Arrest!

"He laid hold of the dragon, that serpent of old, who is the Devil and Satan, and bound him for a thousand years; and he cast him into the bottomless pit, and shut him up, and set a seal on him, so that he should deceive the nations no more till the thousand years were finished..."
Revelation 20:2-3

This is what we need to tell the enemy. Based on solid evidence, the investigation confirms that enemies have been killing the church daily. They have been issued a warrant for their arrest and await trial in the last days, when they stand before the judgment throne. It's time to bind and loose! No matter who they are or what they try and do, bind & loose. The Bible says that God gives us the keys to the kingdom and that whatever we bind on earth He will also bind in heaven, and what so ever we loose on earth it shall be loosed in the heavens. No explanation needed on that part.

Now when you arrest the enemy you can't carry out this mission in any kind of way; you have to be equipped. You have to wear the right clothing and use the necessary weapons.

...

2 Corinthians 10:4, "For the weapons of our warfare are not carnal but mighty in God for pulling down strongholds,"

...

The weapons that we fight with are not carnal but spiritual. This battle we fight is not a natural one, therefore we must war in the spirit. Ephesians tells us that we do not wrestle against flesh and blood but against demonic entities that have been loosed to cause trouble in our lives therefore, we must have the right weapons and clothing.

That's why Paul told us to put on the whole armor of God that we may be able to stand against the enemy, and having done all you could to prepare yourself to stand, JUST STAND! You have to know that God will cover and protect you if you dwell in his secret place. There you find protection under his wings (Psalms 91). If you are in His secret place then you're in His will, and if you're in His will you're in His power, and if you're in His power then you're covered and protected under the authority that resides in the name which is above every name; JESUS!

Now unto him who is able to keep you from falling. To present you faultless, before the presence of his glory; with exceeding Joy. To the only wise God our savior; be glory, and majesty, dominion, and power, both now and forever, Amen!

Cornelius W. Dixon

Cornelius W. Dixon is from Luverne Alabama in the Crenshaw county area. He is a devoted singer, minister, and author; who loves to do whatever he can for the kingdom of God. Cornelius has been a minister for over 12 years now, and the things he writes about; are things he has experienced through his time of ministry. Thank you for all of your love and support, It is definitely a motivation to continue writing and doing the things he loves!

Cornelius Dixon Ministries

For more info on new titles, updates, and booking for Author Cornelius Dixon. Please contact via email:
TheAuthorHimself@gmail.com
or
http://theauthorhimself.wix.com/theauthorhimself

Acknowledgments

It would not be right to close this book without giving out a few flowers!

I would like to give glory, honor and praise to God; for the things he is doing in and around my life. If it had not been for him, leading and guiding me; my ministry would seriously be dead or on life support. I thank him for not giving up on me!

I would like to thank my God-Parents, Mr. Fredrick & Mrs. Devona Jones thank you for always standing by me, and reminding me of how great things are awaiting for me!

I would like to thank my Pastor and church family (St. James Baptist Church, Rutledge AL). Thank you for all of the love and support.

And thank you! My readers, I pray that you have been blessed through the writings God has birth through me! Thank you for your continued support with "Reaching beyond the break" and now this work. I've seriously come too far to stop now, so as God gives to me, I will write more that I may give too you!

Cornelius W. Dixon

The Serial Killer Ministries

Made in the USA
Columbia, SC
28 February 2023